# HAMSTERS

## Questions and Answers

by Christina Mia Gardeski

CAPSTONE PRESS
a capstone imprint

Pebble Plus is published by Capstone Press,
1710 Roe Crest Drive, North Mankato, Minnesota 56003
www.mycapstone.com

Library of Congress Cataloging-in-Publication Data is available on the Library of
Congress website.

ISBN 9781515703525 (library binding) | ISBN 9781515703594 (pbk.) |
ISBN 9781515703655 (ebook (pdf))

**Editorial Credits**
Carrie Braulick Sheely and Michelle Hasselius, editors; Kayla Rossow, designer;
Pam Mitsakos, media researcher; Gene Bentdahl, production specialist

**Photo Credits**
Alamy: imageBROKER, 19, Juniors Bildarchiv GmbH, 5;  Dreamstime: Alexkalashnikov, 11;
iStockphoto: snapphoto, 17; Shutterstock: AlexKalashnikov, 7, cover, DoubleBubble, 1, 22, Jane
September, 21, Steve Design, 13, stock_shot, 15; Thinkstock: DimitrovoPhtography, 9

## Note to Parents and Teachers

The Pet Questions and Answers set supports national science standards related to
life science. This book describes and illustrates hamsters. The images support early
readers in understanding the text. The repetition of words and phrases helps early
readers learn new words. This book also introduces early readers to subject-specific
vocabulary words, which are defined in the Glossary section. Early readers may
need assistance to read some words and to use the Table of Contents, Glossary,
Read More, Internet Sites, Critical Thinking Using the Common Core, and Index
sections of the book.

Printed in China.
022016    007713

# Table of Contents

# Who Has a Mouthful?

My hamster!

Hamsters keep food in
big pouches in their cheeks.
They do not eat the food all
at once. They save it for later.

# Why Is My Hamster Up at Night?

Hamsters sleep during the day. They have lots of energy at night. They chew on toys and spin hamster wheels. Your noisy friend might keep you awake!

# Can Hamsters See in the Dark?

Hamsters cannot see well. They can see less than 6 inches (15.2 centimeters) in front of their noses. They use their whiskers to feel what is around them.

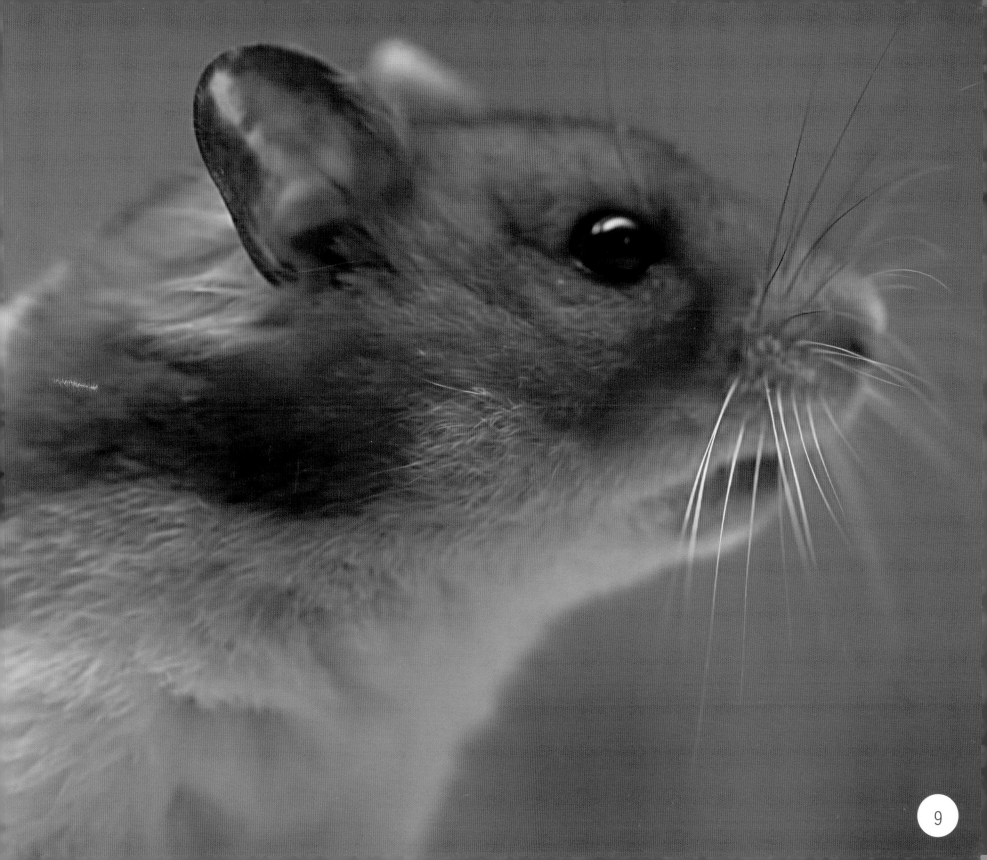

# Where Can I Keep My Hamster?

Most hamsters live alone in a
big cage. Add deep bedding,
a hamster wheel, and toy tunnels.
Keep the cage away from
hot and cold spots and other pets.

# What Do Hamsters Eat?

Hamsters eat dry hamster pellets. They can also eat hamster mix made from seeds, grains, and nuts. They like fruits and vegetables. They drink fresh water from a hanging bottle.

# Why Do Hamsters Dig?

Wild hamsters live in burrows
they dig underground.

Pet hamsters dig in bedding.

They hide food there and sleep.

# Can I Let My Hamster Out of Its Cage?

A free hamster can get lost. Let your hamster run inside a hamster ball away from stairs. Watch it play in a bin of bedding and tubes. Always watch your free hamster closely.

# Can My Hamster Catch My Cold?

Hamsters can get colds from people.

Try not to sneeze or cough

near your hamster.

Wash your hands before

touching it or its food.

# How Long Do Hamsters Live?

Hamsters can live up to three years. Their small bodies can be hurt easily. Be gentle when you play with your hamster.

# Glossary

**bedding**—soft, shredded wood, paper, or other material that can be used for an animal's bed

**burrow**—a tunnel or hole in the ground made or used by an animal

**energy**—the strength to do active things without getting tired

**hamster ball**—an empty ball that a hamster can go inside to run

**pellet**—a small, dry piece of hamster food

**pouch**—a large space in a hamster's cheek used to store food

**underground**—below the ground

**whisker**—one of the long hairs growing on the face and bodies of some animals

# Read More

**Ganeri, Anita.** *Nibble's Guide to Caring for Your Hamster.* Pets' Guides. Chicago: Capstone Heinemann Library, 2013.

**Graubart, Norman D.** *My Hamster.* Pets Are Awesome! New York: PowerKids Press, 2014.

**Hutmacher, Kimberly M.** *I Want a Hamster.* I Want a Pet. North Mankato, Minn.: Capstone Press, 2012.

# Internet Sites

FactHound offers a safe, fun way to find Internet sites related to this book. All of the sites on FactHound have been researched by our staff.

Here's all you do:

Visit *www.facthound.com*

Type in this code: 9781515703525

Check out projects, games and lots more at
**www.capstonekids.com**

# Critical Thinking
# Using the Common Core

1. Hamsters use their whiskers to feel what is around them. What are whiskers? (Craft and Structure)

2. Why do hamsters dig underground and into their bedding? (Key Ideas and Details)

3. If you have a cold, what are some ways you can keep your hamster from getting sick? (Key Ideas and Details)

# Index